Recital
of Love

Recital of Love

Sacred Receivings

Keren Dibbens-Wyatt

PARACLETE PRESS
BREWSTER, MASSACHUSETTS

2020 First Printing

Recital of Love: Sacred Receivings

Copyright © 2020 by Keren Dibbens-Wyatt

ISBN 978-1-64060-406-3

Library of Congress Cataloging-in-Publication Data

Names: Dibbens-Wyatt, Keren, 1971- author.
Title: Recital of love : sacred receivings / Keren Dibbens-Wyatt.
Description: Brewster, Massachusetts : Paraclete Press, 2020. |
Summary: "Written as nuggets of wisdom and encouragement in
poetic prose, each piece gives us an insight into God's heart"
– Provided by publisher.
Identifiers: LCCN 2019046824 | ISBN 9781640604063
ISBN 9781640604070 (mobi)
ISBN 9781640604087 (epub) | ISBN 9781640604094 (pdf)
Subjects: LCSH: Meditations.
Classification: LCC BV4832.3 .D53 2020 | DDC 242–dc23
LC record available at https://lccn.loc.gov/2019046824

10 9 8 7 6 5 4 3 2 1

Published by Paraclete Press
Brewster, Massachusetts
www.paracletepress.com

Printed in the United States of America

To the Living God,
who speaks through his Word,
through his Spirit,
and even deigns to give us good gifts
through weak and broken voices
like mine.
May he be forever praised.

CONTENTS

CONTENTS

And he said to them, "Therefore every scribe who has been trained for the kingdom of heaven is like a master of a house, who brings out of his treasure what is new and what is old."

—Matthew 13:52

The Scriptorium

*I*N THE CAVERNS OF GOD'S HEART, I am sent in prayer.

Am I willing to go deep into wisdom and grace? Here is a cavern, holy and light.

Surrounded by a curtain of water, the roar of his waterfalls.

The water is infinite, it is living water, it does not need to flow to anywhere or return, it just flows down in blessing.

The ground is earthy and hard and covered in eggs, incubated by the warmth that rises from below. They are large, like those of an ostrich.

There are flakes falling gently. They are not ash, but snow—they fizzle away when they touch the ground, releasing steam which is cleansing.

All the elements are present. It feels incredibly holy. I have sandaled feet which are comfortably warm, and the frosty touch of snowflakes now and again on my toes is refreshing.

I sit on a high-backed stool. Before me is a book. It is sacred, it crackles, it feels alive. I am not here to read it, but to write in it. A book of wisdom. It is put together piece by piece and page by page. It is a recitation of love.

Love from the beginning, into the middle, perfected at the end. It is the story of stories, of why everything has the form that it does. It is given into the hands of the mortal for understanding and for the triumph of God's holy grace.

All newness and oldness are here to assist you.

My hands are held out, they are blessed with the kiss of the Christ-King. They will never let you down.

I turn them over to receive a pot of ink, which is everlasting. It will never run out. It is living ink, and it will never betray God's thoughts, meaning, it will not stray from the thoughts of his heart.

A pen also will be given to me. It is made from the feather of an archangel. It will be faithful to its master, the Holy One.

The kiss, the ink, and the quill shall be your guarantee that this mission is from God, and that it cannot be corrupted.

I pray for help, for quiet, space, energy, and freedom from distraction. I am the Lord's humble servant—this all feels so huge, what can I do but say, "Yes, if you help me," and then humanly, knuckle down?

Holy, holy, holy day, this beginning! There is much to say and I do not know where to start. How to fill pages with the love of God?! He will lead me. All is in his hands.

*P*EOPLE SOMETIMES REACT AS IF IT WERE strange that God still speaks to us. But why should one Beloved not speak to another? For what could be more natural than that my Creator should speak to my heart, or yours to your own? What could be more expected than that the Word might continue to express himself, as he has done since time dawned by his command?

Do not be alarmed, dear reader, for I do not claim any special relationship with God, nor do I insist that what is contained in this tiny offering plate of a book are locutions, for they were not given dramatically, but softly in the heart of silent prayer. Nor are the words set down here holy; this is not in any way Scripture, and where there is anything that you feel detours from that dear and beloved book, please stick with the Bible.

I am simply receiving and putting wordy flesh on the bones of thoughts that come unbidden in that place of prayerful openness, as mystics are wont to do. I believe all of this is given by God for sharing, but I acknowledge my own capacity for error and foolishness at the same time. Discernment is vital and must be driven by the Holy Spirit.

After each offering, I have placed the Hebrew word *selah*, which is found mostly in the book of Psalms. It is traditionally held to mean an instruction to pause and reflect, and I feel that it is good to do just this—to stop and savour what we have just read before carrying on—exactly as we might take a moment between mouthfuls of rich food.

Sometimes I refer to God using traditional terms such as Lord, Father, or using male pronouns, sometimes with a female image such as a mother. These are just a matter of convenience, as, of course, the Trinity both encompasses and exceeds all our ideas and definitions of gender and relationship. Please do not let my narrow use of these terms make you feel excluded from hearing that beloved voice.

Likewise, be assured that God never shows us things to condemn us, but rather to help us see more clearly how we might love him, ourselves, and others better. If he speaks to us of hardness of heart, for instance, it is to gift us with an opportunity to come to him and soften.

I give you this small book then, as a voice calling in the wilderness that few visit, and my only claim for it is that these words are dear to my heart as from my Beloved, and kept like love letters to remind me of what love speaks, and to keep that desire aflame.

Light

VERY SPARK OF LIGHT, every small particle that illuminates, this is the love, the very heart of God, speaking light and joy over the world. The shining of water reveals the true nature of creation, to reflect. We reflect for his glory, both the light that is contained in every piece of air and sky, and the love of the heart that turns to its maker every minute of every day. How such a heart, given to God, will flutter and warm with turning, constant turning, back to him and away from the mire of the world!

For every turning is a manifestation of Grace and is holy and pure. Purity is misunderstood, but it fires like a dart at God's heart. Whenever a glance, a thought, a longing, aims itself towards God and towards the will and intentions of God's heart, there is purity, there is holiness. This holiness attracts and receives of itself, like a magnet retrieves metal. Holiness draws the holy and sacred, the good and the glorious, into itself, all returning to the place of its birth. And light is the same, reflecting back to itself over and over again so that it exists in waves as well as particles, always and ever showing the way to God and coming home to him. Let the world fall away.

Selah

Silence

*W*HEN THE HAILSTONES COME, hot and heavy, the silence falls too, between each orb. The silence of falling air is louder to my ears than the clattering of ice. The silence is white and deep and broad. It covers everything in an avalanche of purity. All is covered, mantled in the glory of silence. Noise especially. For where noise is, there is a covering surround of silence, or the noise would not sound. Where the dark is, the light waits to engulf it. Where the chaos is, the order waits to redeem it. Where the sound is, the silence waits also, patiently to cascade and descend, to flow into every corner and around every obstacle.

Just as there is more air in a jar of marbles than there is glass, or more space in a handful of sand than there is silicon, so there is more silence in a cacophony than there is noise. Listen for it, look for it, let it become the language of your heart: not a strange other tongue, but as natural to you as any speech.

For silence and space is what gives my universe her shape, what defines her, and it would be well for my prophets and people to become acquainted with these things, the building blocks of creation. Make friends therefore, with emptiness, and come to know nothing, and you will be full to bursting with new life and sated by wonder.

Silence is charged with, rings with, the power of the unsaid. It gathers it in, pulls it, condenses around it until it must be unleashed as song—released into creative acts. When empty it begins again, reloading, discharging, like a pupil constantly dilating, or a flower opening and closing. Like the ventricles of a beating heart. Like the very breath of God.

Selah

Seed

SEED IS HOW LIGHT ENTERS THE WORLD. Life is made up of pods and cases, wombs, and soft bellies full of newness. Here is my melting pot of creativity, where tiny fish and elegant gazelles alike, peas and wayward souls are fashioned. All is spiralled into form, by light and texture, home and free, made never to be unmade, created for life through death. For all such casings are finite and limited in time.

All eggshells will be cracked open to let life leak out and be born into the air. Each life must leave its cocooned beginnings and breathe the free air I have provided. There are no exceptions to this in my will. For it is not death that you are created for, though you will all pass through it, but for life—life in all its full abundant richness that you will enter and for which you were destined and designed from the first spark—for the universe of love in its full and whole spectrum, every colour expanding to bursting point, like a proud heart full of daddy-love.

There are no restraints here, no smallness of feeling, no holding back. Tides of emotion run deep and true and allow themselves the liberty of touch and devotion, of expressing the grace of God. There is no stiff upper lip stifling of your true emotions with me. I would rather you stamped and raged, toddler-tantrum fist-pumping frustration explosions than stood before me in a calmly exteriored containment of lava. Pour it out and be done with it.

By the same token, let me in, ask me to inhabit every emotion, every hurt, every tired muscle and aching bone, every weary blood cell that will have me, and I will make my home there too. For nothing can hold my greatness, but I can shine it abroad, like the refraction of light from the purest source. There is nowhere it cannot reach, and all life begins from my shining.

Travesties are places where my light seems thwarted, held back, shut out by the blackout curtains of stubborn hearts. Surround yourselves then with givers of light and not keepers of the dark who will try to persuade you that you can exist cut off from me, from your source, from the Light.

Selah

Triumph

*T*RIUMPH IS NOT THE WINNING AGAINST BUT the winning through. It is the making it to the other side, jumping off the rope swing and looking back, breathless and ruddy-cheeked in glee. It is the deep sigh that says, "It did not stop me!" We can triumph broken, not bitter; crushed, not dismembered. Triumph bears the standard of love held high, looked up to; the light shines from our banners and glints off the weapons we used in brightness, the glare alone enough to send enemies scurrying.

For understand this: there is no victory without me. Without me all is empty shell, open casket, pale and cold. Victory with me is given with shouts of joy and no bloodletting. It is worked with cries and trumpet calls, but also patient sitting and dull waiting. Glory looks decidedly different close up.

Here in my heart, the very definitions of words are changing, coming face-to-face with their own inadequacy. For the spoils of war are given from my hand, not looted, and the lands passed on to those I deem worthy, my trust-friends and confidantes. The good earth is given as territories to those who will husband it with tender hearts and soiled hands.

I eschew the rich and the powerful who do not want to get their hands dirty or their hearts broken.

For my people are the broken in heart and the crushed in spirit, the low and the humble, who tend their own roots before pruning the branches of others, and their soft, brittle wondering warms my heart. These are my beloved dear ones, the lost and confused, the uncertain and the wounded. Dismiss them at your peril, for you send me away with them! If you want to find me, look here first, among the discarded and bereft, and do not speak to me of rewards and revival until you have lived a time in their love.

I take no prisoners, no tepid self-servers who will not give me their whole hearts. I am in the business of freedom and completion, redemption and blessing. Your boldness will not serve you here. Remember your knees and what they are for. When you can bend, you will rise my children. Remember your neck and what it is for; when its stiffness can bow, then your heads will be lifted lovingly. This is my way, dusty and true. Walk in it.

Selah

Diamonds

IAMONDS AMONG MEN, WOMEN, and children are those who seek me out by seeking the good and humble hearts in themselves and others. For it is the childlike, pure-souled and helpless who can truly see goodness. The clever judge everything and think themselves wise. The wicked see only what might profit them, and the strong lambast anyone who tries to offer them aid or succour.

Do you see, my beloved, how much these things impede the flow of my kingdom? Therefore, seek not the smart, the selfish or the self-sufficient, for in their hearts and minds they are already saved and healed, whole and presumptuous in their perfection, when the reality is far from this.

This is what is meant by "if you lose your life you will gain it," for it is only those who speak of their own unworthiness who become worthy, and only those who give up their hearts willingly who can truly love the world into submission.

I love everyone with an equal and unmatched passion, which even the universe balks at. Do not mistake this or think otherwise. But it is only the few who walk into that love by becoming small enough in their own eyes, who will be utterly enveloped by love in this life.

More is to come, of course, but I do not wish to speak of this yet, for I am like a parent on Christmas Eve who has hidden all the best presents and will relish the giving out on our special day, when there shall be hands clapped in glee and unscheduled dancing from the heart, mine and yours, and the floor of heaven shall rock with happy laughter!

See, I can hardly contain the vision of it, even within myself! But for now, the seedlings must grow to be trained in the Way. I am the Good Gardener, and I may be trusted with all things, from the care of the tiniest wind-blown seed to the mightiest, most ancient of oaks.

Place everything in my hands in prayer, therefore, and like all good under-gardeners, toil and watch and wait. The diamonds are growing. I can hear them sing.

Selah

Time

TIME IS NOT THE THING YOU THINK IT IS. Time is expansive and elastic. It is there to enable and enlarge, not to constrict and confine. Time is your helpmeet, for it divides the day into hours of prayer, of meeting, of work, play, challenge, and rest, and the night into a silent hopeful darkness for denizens of moon-gazing, star-watching, birthing of wisdom. A time for doers, a time for dreamers. Lines may be crossed over or mixed up, yet time remains the same: a watchman on the towers of your life who proclaims the coming of the dawn and the dusk, who sings you into prayers and death alike. But though time seems rigid and preset, it is pegged out as the boundary of an encampment, and the more you savour it, the further the rope reaches.

If you take no notice of the markers I have placed, you will trip over them before you see them and lie face down in the dust, hot and confused, wondering at your own ignorance of the obvious.

Time is the Good Shepherd's sheepdog, a Border Collie who will herd and guide you, if you know how to respond to her presence, and recognize as she does, the sound of my voice and the pitch of my whistle. Be wise therefore and learn the ways of edges and guidelines, of drooping eyelids and weary backs, of aching heads and sore knees, of overworked hands. For all these are shepherdings into rest, and my fold awaits you always, a place of replenishment and safety, love and restoration.

Visit often and let the grass grow green and lush for your readiness, and your jaws rest from the grind.

Selah

Prayer

*B*USYNESS MUST ALWAYS MAKE WAY FOR PRAYER and not the other way around. We cannot shoehorn prayer into our day as if it were another thing to cross off the list. For prayer is not something you do, it is something beautiful that happens in your heart, a fluttering burst of coloured wings soaring up to their maker when they hear his voice in the stillness. A flock of songbirds returning to their mother, who is calling them up to higher branches.

Prayer is always a homecoming, a place where desires find their true voice and character and are not what you thought they were. Where desperations are met with tear-brimming eyes full of compassion and mercy.

Prayer is a reaching up and out, a wondering, not-knowing, questioning, angry demand for demonstration sometimes, met with loving hands closing around your tantrumming fist. A wailing and a gnashing of teeth, hell brought before heaven's throne, looking for answers and finding them.

For no one goes away from my table hungry. Did I not speak? Did I not answer you? Was the air crackling with the un-saidness of my words? Does this silence all around your pain let the naysayers creep in, telling you to 'curse God and die', be done with it, admit the non-existence of I AM, or the not-caring of love itself, the lies told by the truth of the Word? This is folly, and child's talk, the babbling of fools in the marketplace, of gossips at the city gate.

How can the one who created ears not hear? Or the one who gave you sight, not see everything? Nothing is hidden from me. Your words and longings, your heart cries, your situations of need, arise before me tenfold. I know all. The softest unspoken whisper of disappointment rises alongside the loudest birth-pain groaning.

I will respond. I AM response. Relationship is what I do.

Do not be dismayed. For who are you to know when legions of angels have been dispatched on your behalf, or a journey set in motion, or a healing balm called for?

I alone have all the answers, and in me you must place your confidence and your trust. Your hearts are mine and I care prodigiously, painfully for each one. Life is not a game. I take serious things seriously.

But know this. I will not answer your whining or your selfish disdain of others, your foolish prattling and your skin-deep wants. For I know you better than you know yourself and I will give you only good gifts.

I sense what you need, even before you part your lips to speak, but I like to hear your voice and I want to spend time with you. So, chatter if you will, but speak to me also heart to heart and spirit to Spirit and make friends with the holy silence of listening and being still.

For it is in awareness that I am to be found, smiling kindly on all things, with the fullness of compassion and tenderness only a constantly breaking heart can give.

Selah

Stillness

STILLNESS IS NOT AN ENFORCED POSITION. I make no one go there solely of my volition or against theirs. Like silence, and the listening that makes it come alive, stillness is a place of discovery. It teaches who I am and you are not. It enables you to notice. There is glory and goodness all around, in every atom, every whisper of the wind, every creature's song.

Here in the paying attention of doing nothing is where you will find me, if you find me anywhere. Not in your heart or soul, not in a voyage of self-discovery or enlightenment, but by casting out the grandiose and sitting in stillness. Here everything worthwhile is louder, brighter, more evident.

Giving up your masks and your illusion of control, admitting you live in a universe beyond your feeble understanding, this is the place to begin to know me. For which of you could manufacture one sparrow's wing? Or the perfect spiral of a snail's shell, grown over time to be trampled on gleefully by the unthinking? Could you make one stalk, one blade of grass, in all its intricacy? Can you create life and greening? Or is it I who do this?

Sitting in the silent running of stillness this question is not difficult to answer. For here you must face the truth of your inadequacies, and the yearning in your heart for something, someone, greater than yourself. Instead of wanting to know, you will want there to be someone who knows. Instead of desiring control, you will want someone greater, someone kinder, someone magnificent to be in control. You will see how much further beyond you everything is—further than you ever imagined. Further than they ever taught you in school or in church. For it is one thing to think you can cast mountains into the sea (whoever did this, and might you lower yourself to metaphor?), but quite another to remove specks from eyes.

In the stillness you will see how much the smallness of things matters, how much I care for each one. Life is an expression of being—my being, my wisdom, my glory—and in the stillness you will start to peek round corners at yourself and see your tiny part in it all. You will not balk at your own smallness, for such it is. You will learn only to acknowledge it before me. This is what saved Job, this insight, this perception of God and his creation. Once you begin to acknowledge, to accept what I am capable of, what I have done, what I am doing, what I might choose to do, and with what forethought, care, and precision, with what wisdom and love, with what truth, beauty, and reckless abandon, encased in beautiful order I do it, then you will trust me and begin to know me and seek me out.

And it is here we begin, in almost totally losing sight of yourself, one tree in a plethora of forested worlds, looking beyond to the Source of Life.

Selah

Spirit

DOES THE SPIRIT ALIGHT ON YOUR HAND like the most delicate lace-winged creature, startled by the slightest sound or movement? No, that is not how it is. For when the Spirit makes her home within you, she is anchored to your very soul, like the roots of a tree that cannot be pulled out. She becomes part of you, and you my dwelling place.

This partnership is strong and requires great force to break. It is a source of enabling. She moves in your life according to my mysteries and yet remains bound to me, an expression of the love between us all: between her and me, for we are, along with our Christ child, One; and between you and me, for we are also soulmates and beloved family members.

Therefore, do not mistake this relationship as weak, fragile, or easily shattered. For a cord of three strands is not easily broken, and no unwinding is done except to release the captives and set them free. The roots of the spirit of love grow deep and tortuous, long and intimately entrenched. My love does not flee from you so easily.

Allow her tendrils to dig down, and let these roots wrap around your heart, exploring each chamber of feeling. She never obstructs, but only enraptures, soothes, holds fast to the goodness she carries everywhere as a reflection of me. She brings my DNA joyfully to your every cell, infusing your thoughts with mine, keeping my heart in yours. A connection beating time together.

Let her be welcome and let her warm your heart, teach your knowing places, and make you a temple of my delicious dwelling, where living water flows and the Spirit breathes joy and holy laughter. All of it bubbles up and through in irrepressible goodness: joy, hope, love, mercy: all this is the gentle gurgling of a child of God.

Selah

Waves

$\mathcal{T}$HE SEA OF LOVE, so wide and deep and rolling, any perceived horizon so distant, the east removed from the west as far as arms on a cross of wood might be stretched in the compassionate embrace of a broken world, a thirsty land which is given only saltwater and cups of vinegar to drink. Here is an ocean of freshness poured out from the clouds of heaven and rolling towards my people.

Who are my people but the ones who see the waves and welcome them? For living water knocks on the door of each life, and all must either open or remain closed. Opening yourself lets the life flood in, washes all things clean, constantly beginning over and over, and refreshes each space. Water does not care what shape you are, what colours paint you, what has gone before, what you used to be; your gender, race, countrymen are nothing to me in this rolling out of liquid love. Only receive and be blessed and learn that your feet will never be dry again. You will always walk ankle deep in my mercy and be anchored on my shore of hopes.

But for those who keep the door tightly shut, there is only the misery of sandbags and the standing for hours with digits in holes to try to hold back the force of love. They may sit Canute-like and imagine their kingdoms reach beyond their own thresholds, but they are wrong.

I live by hoping they will allow a trickle in under the door now and again and maybe taste and see that I am good, and that my loving water is pure and delicious. There is a whole freshwater ocean available! Can they not see that it is better to be drowned in my love than lost in a dry desert of misery and self-containment? Here they make their own dry and dusty rules and stick to them, like the story told of a preposterous old king gripping the arms of his beached throne, proclaiming and declaring the authority he claims from heaven, but a heaven he does not know, for it has never entered his heart. How sad and how curious is a man!

For this is something my women may hold in gratitude, that as the water bearers they know the gift of life when they see it. No more carrying jars of heavy clay on their heads, filled to the brim now instead as living jars.

But for the rich and the privileged this truth is harder and their borderlands tougher to let go. Ah, but what they miss out on! Will someone help me tell them? Can the message of love's oceans be carried to them on the crest of wording white waves and by the reaching out of those already filled to overflowing?

I hope between us, we shall flood the world with love, and a new kind of deluged drowning, edged with rainbows, will occur, along with rebirth to life in all its fullness, only once we have experienced being lost in the waves of almighty love.

Selah

Shining

*S*HINING MY LIGHT INTO THE WORLD REQUIRES only one thing of you: that you gaze at me. For how shall you reflect the light if you do not first receive and perceive it? No, it must be there, glowing in your face, firing in your heart, reaching out to others like a beam of love. My love-light is sacred and pure, and it is recognizable everywhere in the world: my universal language, a helping hand and a smiling face within a world of trouble. This is how people will know you are my followers, by the reflection you show of me.

Good works are many and varied and not prescribed by anyone but me. So yours shall be set before you. Therefore, do whatever work you are given, whatever lies before you, with my love-light clearly visible. Stay constant to me in your gaze, in your adoration, in your belonging, in your giving of yourself, and all else will fall into its rightful and holy place.

Do not be dismayed if the work seems lowly, or indeed if it lifts you higher than you desire to go. Accept your situation as of my making, for if you love me, there also am I, even among the pots and pans. Ask for grace and strength and wisdom, and then shine, turning and dancing in your love of me and in my love of the world,

so that my love-light plays across every face in wonder, every page in truth, every dirty dish in transformation. For in my light everything and every task is made simple and beautiful.
Selah

Beyondness

*T*HERE IS MUCH, so much more to be said than can ever be said. Words are inadequate for most of what needs to be poured out from my heart to the world. And so, I do not only speak, but sing, and the flowers and birds add colour and harmony. For I am speaking out an endless stream of universes and laughing worlds into existence. Chains of constellations form from the breath expelled from my nostrils! You truly have no concept or words for the wonder and vastness that I am, nor for the longings in my heart, or the love I harbour, even for the tiniest harvest mouse.

I am beyond all knowing. Do not fence me in, therefore, with your words and ideas, but stretch out with your heart-mind and sense instead, with your feelings, the vibrations of compassion and creation that echo through all of time and space, that resound in your own one tiny life.

By all means, chase my glory, watch my ways, gaze at my goodness, know my presence in the stillness of the waiting heron and the swish of a goldfish's tail. But do not expect, no, never expect to see more than a glimmer of the whole, more than a flicker of light, more than the furthest edge of the universes of my being. You can only catch a trail of stardust, as you gape in open-mouthed awe at my Love and my Being.

You will return home, but for now you are crammed in the rock cleft with Moses as your guide, and you will only sense my passing, unable to comprehend it.

Yet, do not be dismayed! There is enough in this one moment to keep your minds and hearts busy for all eternity, if you truly love me. Think, ponder, write and paint, sculpt and garden, love and worship, sing and compose, set my wonders into stone and colour and rhyme, do these things with my blessing. But do them knowing that all you have seen is the smallest corner of the hem of my trailing robe, galaxies caught up in the stitching, or that what you capture in your words, or your gleaning of imagery is minuscule, and so small a part of who I am.

Because I exist wholly and holy throughout all creation, every quark knows my name. I may be found under the tiniest pebble, or beneath the lark's tongue. But if you spy me there, do not imagine for one moment that I am wholly discovered. You could live a thousand years and not see. Gaze instead at my reflection, given within your own heart, and sing with it of my love—for here is where we begin our journey back to unity.

Selah

Smile

*T*IME TO QUESTION YOUR BELONGINGS, your allegiances. To whom do you owe your duty and love? To the world, which you believe feeds and clothes you, and which laps up your every word and laughs in all the right places? Which lays seeming treasure at your well-shod feet? Or to the Lord of Hosts, who made you, who breathed life into your modelled clay? For in your muddled mind you believe the world sustains you, and yet owes you worship and adulation.

You believe God to be distant and ambivalent, as though it were the world that truly loved you! As though what you call science (your own knowing of my ways) knitted your DNA together alone in some cosmic laboratory, as if all life were cold and clinical, explicable and clean.

Worship instead the God of light and mercy, foolish ones! The God who rules over mess and disarray, who finds the sliver of gold in the dung heap and the silver needle in the haystack, the God who sees you for who you are in all your imperfection and loves you still, with a good mother's love, absorbed in the smile you once had, and may yet choose to bestow upon her again. She waits, longing and loving, caring and not-counting the cost, and yet you dismiss her time and time again, heading off instead to adventures on the seven sinful seas; a pirate on a ship that sails blasted by ill winds and pulled by earthly tides, when you could be safely ensconced and beloved in heaven's harbour!

Weary am I of waiting, and yet determined, not with gritted teeth or an expression set in stone, but with aching heart and soft, heaving tears. Sail home to me, my dear children, and be suckled, redeemed, renewed, made gentle in my image and sent on new voyages of discovery where we shall travel together into seas of starlight, scaling moonbeams and navigating the eddying edges of galaxies, cresting the brink of each new dimension as it is birthed from my song.

Come first to these other shores and leave the hard-as-iron, caustic, cold world of counting and proving grounds behind. Come find your true worth in me. Find it in the softness of my arms and the rolling laugh of my belly as you smile on me again.

Selah

Stone

*I*MPERVIOUS TO ALL THINGS STANDS THE HEART of stone. Unwilling to bend, it cannot delight in the daisies clamouring for attention around its feet. It does not imagine even for a second that it is wanted or loved, that others long to see it come alive. Instead its only goal is protection, armour, hardness. And what does it surround but more stone? For the heart of stone is weary and cold, sad and lonely.

The loving cure stands near and smiling, but it will not heed.

Oh, heart of stone, you allow the moss and lichen to grow, but despise their cheerfulness and life!

It calls all who surround it parasites, not realizing that they are trying to bring it to life, not leech it away. For there is no warmth or sap to be found here, only more cold, impenetrable stone. The flesh has long since stopped beating, and its pink and warm softness been calcified into a stalwart of certainties, intellect, and a despising of those who breathe.

And yet, here still the lion may stop and stare for a moment, resting his golden gaze on a lifeless form; deeply, purposefully exhaling, and melting the statue of a heart until it stretches its muscles, sighs with remembrances of blood, and starts to reclaim itself as living tissue. Craggy corners fall away, and helping hands brush softened chalk and sandstone until the heart, marbled with pulsing life, sets eyes on the Way again. A final roar to seal the covenant and embed the memories into true identity, and padding paws leap away, a new heart bounding with them.

Selah

Veil

THE CHAMBERS BETWEEN OUR HEARTS have grown dark and misty. There is an over-clouding inside each one, where the cataracts have formed over ages, making a veil between the vision of my heart and yours. A barrier that needs to be cracked, like a sheet of ice formed between dimensions.

The curtain of fog descended when you turned away from me. When you chose your heart over mine. Your small being over my I AM far-reaching existence. When you chose to bury yourself in material things and gave up flying.

Only your hot tears of return will melt the divide between us. Only the warm breath of your longing for my love. Only the ringing out of your singing praise will shatter this sheet of frozen gaping.

The springtime of our love will then begin! The flowers will return to my halls, and the chambers will be decked with vines, dripping with fruit, laden with birdsong, heavy with the promise of wine.

Come then, cry your way home, feel your deep yearnings, sing me your songs of desire and adoration. Be utterly mine and find yourself saturated by all the love the universe has to offer, a pleasing home in my dwelling place, safe in the womb of my heart, together again.

Selah

Feet

*T*HOSE OF YOU WHO ENJOY MY SUNSHINE and showers more than others, do not worry! The peaks and troughs of your existence are not eternal. You will keep your balance if the eyes of your heart remain fixed on me. I do not bring you troubles in order to chastise, nor do I douse your parade, or pull the rug from under you like a spiteful child.

These twists and turns, these are different surfaces you need to learn to walk upon, wilds and waters that must know the imprint of your feet before you can cope with the carpet of heaven which is loud and full of life. Too much for baby feet! They must be calloused and mile-weary to walk in my outer courts.

So I say again, do not despair or worry, instead take the honour that is given and ride the learning curve meandering before you. If you take it in my stride, then the seven-league sacred boots you receive to dance and leap across my kingdom will be easy wearing for you, because as my children you must glide over failure and success, seeing them for what they are, and only prize my loving presence and living water. It flows from my overrunning heart-fountain of loving-kindness-mercy-grace which is so golden in its goodness and glory that you have no words that can describe it!

Oh, here you will leap and bound like gazelles and turn on a pinhead! Oh, here you will dance the divine dance of love, with your seasoned soul-soles, and the floors of valleys will rise up and the floors of mountains bow down to meet your joyful feet!

Selah

Rose

*I*F YOU PLUCK A ROSE AND PLACE IT IN A VASE of daisies, it will be ashamed of its thorns and diminished by its height, so aware of its own differences and overwhelmed by the longing to be the same as those around it, that it will shrink before your very eyes.

For it to bloom and open fully, letting light and colour into every dark fissure of its petals, it must be planted in good soil. For my sunshine-love-light to find its way round every petalled corner and into the hidden crevices that frame beauty in curves of darker hue, it must have love whispered to it daily.

It must be taught to open to the dew, to the rain and the sun alike, to become tender to cheek, snail, and aphid, as well as to shining droplets and warm rays.

Open then, to everything, for all things hold a lesson and all wisdom is precious, and there is no full bloom without the courage to face worms. Each rose must find its true form and colour, its own dear shape and vibrant translucency.

And I will shine here and bloom in your blooming. My rose garden spreads fragrance throughout the world, and nothing else smells so sweetly of heaven.

Selah

Ladder

*L*ADDERS ARE FOR CLIMBING DOWN AS WELL as up. For coming back down to earth as well as thinking you can scale the heights. So, climb my ladder, my sweet children, and find as my servant Jacob did that the best way to go is towards the ground, and rest your weary heads on the stones you find there.

Some stairways to heaven are simply mirages, crumbling to nothing once you turn your back on them, and others are all the more sturdy for snaking downwards. Both kinds will appear when you are at your least surefooted, waiting to claim the small, restless hours of the night.

Yet all your wrestling and fighting, your twists and turns, your struggling against me, will end in soft kisses and slight limps, the wetness of cheeks sore from crying, streaks of salt down your face and eyes red from long nights of doubting.

Be assured, I am here, always here, waiting at ground level, sat smiling cross-legged on the good soil, on the dust from which I formed you. Heaven will come soon enough, but it begins here, on the level.

Selah

Fathom

ATHOMING IS UNNECESSARY, MY LOVES. Do not waste your energy and strong minds on measuring depths which are endless. Your plumb lines mean nothing here. Trust me to know that my eternal depths are beyond your counting and the feeding out hand over hand of miles of weighted cord!

Instead of trying to calculate the height and breadth of love, dive into the refreshing water and learn to breathe love again, as you once did. Return, like fish, to your ocean breeding grounds and leap and soar in the water that courses with life.

Counting here is counterintuitive; it makes no sense. For who would hold a ruler along the edge of infinity? Stand back instead and be in awe of the unmeasurable ways of my heart and the unfathomable depths of the universe. Let its love surround you at my behest: my love that I have breathed into every particle of life and every droplet of sea and space. Enjoy being amazed!

Selah

Headgear

*M*Y LIGHT SHINES FROM THE GLORY of your heads in different ways at different times. So, it is important what you place on your heads. Not the battered old hat of a tramp, of one who finds himself worthless and lost, always bowed and bent in supplication; nor a crown of thorns of your own making, fashioned out of needless suffering or of difficulties you have made into idols.

The crowns I have made ready to place on your heads are far different than you imagine, my dearest children! They are light and easy garlands of flowers, fragrant and beyond beautiful. Or they are elegant coronets of gold and diamonds, which you think yourselves unworthy of, yet what else might behove the sons and daughters of a King?

Do not be surprised, then, to find yourselves wreathed in the glory of meadows or encircled in golden light, in the dancing of diamond lights. These things were made for you and there is no mistake. Wear your crowns with pride.

Selah

Temptation

*T*EMPTATION COMES, AS IT WILL, from time to time, and the trick is to disown it before the gates of your heart, so it cannot hope to enter them. See it off straight away, chase it with the broom of righteousness, like an ever-watchful homemaker, keeping your doorstep free of its wiles and dirt. For it will come in guises and with shiny baubles to distract you, sticking its foot in the door like a wicked-witch-queen apple sales rep, salivating at the commission it will earn as you bite into the succulent poisoned morsels it brings.

Do not succumb to the sales patter, the bright incessant chattering, the winks and charms, the laugh that is so false it doesn't stop for breath, and the smile that is somehow just that bit wider than its head. All is falseness, noise, and pitch. You do not need what is offered, you already have all that you need in your own orchard: a place of soft, sweet fruit, home-grown and delicious, angel food wrapped in dull, bumpy skins, perfect in their goodness and imperfections.

For all things real and good are marked by suffering, and will somewhere bear the scars. A pimpled, mottled, lumpy skin, patchy and not fit for television, will taste as golden delicious as any other, more so for being unwaxed, unjudged, and grown in your own backyard.

Speak then of sweetness already found, already known, the treasures within already discovered, and laugh at those who tell you to look elsewhere, at those who would have you travel to far-flung fruit trees; for your destination is always me, and I am already home, here with you, sweet enough.

Selah

Beach

*T*IME IS NOT YOUR ENEMY, BUT YOUR FRIEND. Roll around in it, reach out your arms, and stretch to its very edges. Feel the places where heaven pours in its golden glory, and stick close by. For my people and their lives are portals for the goodness of God. Through them courses my holy manna, nectar-honey milk-love given for the satisfaction of my children. And time was built for this to be welcomed and enjoyed.

All beauty, wisdom, truth, and love cascade through, from deep to deep, calling out, roaring in the pouring of waterfalls and the rolling of breakers over your head and onto the beach of my ever-dwelling love.

For here was where I cooked breakfast for you, and we broke bread again and we spoke truthfully to one another of the things in our hearts, of our yearnings and scars, of our pain and our rising hopes, of our devotion to one another. And here is where you will always be brought back, for here is where you constantly begin again, turning the tide of thoughts and worries, so that they become lost and then transformed in my smiling radiance, into thankfulness, patience, and belonging.

Do not rush away when the world calls to you, but hearken instead to my voice. Stay awhile, eat, soften, and place your trembling, anxious, hand, wrinkled with time and worries, on my chest, and feel the beating of my heart in time with yours— for here all time begins and ends, and serves only me.

Selah

Shepherds

*S*HEPHERDS ARE ALWAYS PORTRAYED AS ragamuffins, dull, and poor, coming in from the cold, confronted (or contrasted) with the great and wise magi in their bejewelled robes. But my truth is very different. For the magi came later, and were bedraggled after the longest journey, and there was nothing at the humble home to give them sustenance, no feasting or fresh clothing, there was only my glory shining, which they took away on their faces, never needing replenishment.

But the herds (and their herders), my people, my flock, were there at the very beginning and being nearer the earth and her ways, their humility in the face of the Christ child was quicker to come and already familiar, calling to something in their protective hearts. For here was the Good Shepherd, and they were for the first time able to feel themselves as a flock. To stop the guard duty of care for just a few glorious hours, and be kept safe, watched over by angels of mercy and the Lord of Lords, albeit as a babe. They were dumbstruck by their own watching of an innocent lamb who was nevertheless King of all shepherds.

Oh, how I love to turn things the right way up when you have made them upside down with your hierarchies and your echelons! I always begin at the beginning, at the bottom, with shepherds warm in fleece jackets, at home near the mangers, comfortable in the presence of a God they could finally relate to, yet before whom their strong knees and sturdy crooks bent and bowed in wonder. Faces wrinkled by the sun, creased in smiles and tears before my Son, not befuddled wretches with no understanding, but my children, meeting their brother for the first time, appreciative and humble, and wiser than many who were to come after.

Selah

Splinters

*C*HIPS OF WOOD FLYING UP INTO UNPROTECTED eyes, but there is no pain, no scream, no understanding of the wound that chopping wood creates. Instead we think, "Oh, this is nothing," or "This is how it is," "I see perfectly, myself," "I need no medical attention," "I have 20/20 vision and I am right about everything, can't you see?"

But the woodcutter knows well his game, as he gleefully swings his axe and another tree in the garden falls to the ground, the knowledge of Good and Evil sent splintering across the world into human sight everywhere. For this is living, sapient wood, and it grows into planks daily, and it grows so large it is a wonder we can keep our balance as we walk along so blinded.

The Lord says, "I am here, come to me, and I will show you the way." And we say, "Don't be silly, why should I need to be shown? I can see perfectly well," and we stumble along blindly, Magoo-like into the next war, the next fracas, the next paltry argument with our neighbour or our spouse.

We argue even with our own souls, the blindness affecting even our inner eye, lost to us and untrained. Oh, we know evil all right and we follow it gladly, never thinking that we are unseeing, but leading the blind gallantly over cliffs of our own making.

"Come to me, all you lost and unseen. Come to me, all you blinded by your own ignorance. Come to me when something glints like lost treasure in the corner of your eye, at the edges, the horizon of your vision, and you want to see it more clearly. I will show you. I have the antidote for the poison. I have the ability to raise your hands to the plank, so you can take it out and be set free. I am the Way, the Truth, and the Life. Come and see."

Selah

Souls

YOUR SOULS ARE SAFE, hidden in me, deeply buried in the flesh of my heart, surrounded by the red mass of all my muscular tenderness. Your souls are safe. The very centre of you is kept and held in the very centre of me. We are already one, and all you need do is find your way home by the realization and the clicking of ruby heels, knowing that you are and were and will be here all the time.

It is not that this life is an illusion or a test, nor that your bodies are separate or unimportant, for flesh matters and all is a part of the whole, but simply that the ending of you will be a beginning and that you shall cast off your skin like one casts off one's coat in joyfully arriving home.

I am your dwelling place. Your souls float like silver ships with sails of gossamer inside the chambers of my eternal love, free, easy, and surrounded by the skies and oceans of abundance, the infinite height and breadth and depth of my glory-goodness-loving-kindness, living and moving and having your being in me.

Here your soul-ships dance and soar, tack and glide. Can you not feel the wind in your face and the laughter gloriously gurgling up to meet your smiles?

Come home, my loves, come flying with abandon, come back to where you always were, and be known, skimming across unbridled freedom and caught up in the thermals and tides of unquenchable Love. I await you, even as I wrap around your already-here-ness.

Selah

Leaves

*L*EAVES ARE FOR TURNING. But some we linger on, or turn back to, or reread, because they have a hold on our hearts, somehow, for good or for ill. Memories are to be treasured, and hurts to be healed.

Savour the sights and smells of the good, but return to the bad only for processing; for allowing the courage to rise that you need to slam the book shut and remove the bookmark from that page. Yes, there is shadow work, but your focus must be on the light, your standing must be at the stones you have erected to lean upon in good times and bad, to memories of my being your very present help in time of need. These are the places in your head to turn back to. May they glow strong and fierce in your history, so that there is no danger of forgetting.

Savour these times, when I was your rescuer, your life, the spark of your inspiration, the defender of your faith and the sustainer of your very soul. Roll these times around your tongue and remember how they tasted, how the bitterness faded completely, and only sweetness remained. For I, the Lord your God, am the God of good things, of sweetness, not of bile, of nectar, not of venom, but of bubbling spring water and golden honey-love, not the acrid burning or the gagging cloying of chalk or staleness. This is no falsely sweetened medicine nor sickly syrup. All that comes from me is pleasant; know it to be so, taste, and see that I the Lord am good!

Selah

Winds of Change

*C*HERRY BLOSSOM FALLS, blown on the wind like skydiving ballerinas to who knows where. But I know. I see and approve of every gust of wind that moves over the earth and nurtures the young into movement or nudges old life over the edge into death. This for you is drama, but for me it is only transformation from one state into another. Change comes hard and fast or softly and barely perceived, but always it comes, and I always see it before you do.

So, do not fret over what is next, who you are becoming, where we are going, what will or won't happen. For all is seen and understood long before you have had the foresight to begin worrying about it!

There is nothing outside of my remit or beyond my notice. I am here and now as in all things, always, and my presence alone should comfort you. If I call you to leap from a branch you will find the spiralling breeze there ready to carry your twirling, petalled form safely to the ground, or be blown to the four winds if I need you to be north-west-east and south all at the same time. It is not for you to worry about. Not because you should not care for yourself, but because you can trust me to care far more than you could ever do. I have everything in hand, and every wind of change is breathed from my Spirit on my order, whether it brings a new season or a sharp shove. Therefore, do not fear the currents in the air, nor the eyes of storms. It is all mine and you are held deeply precious within the centre of my loving will.

Selah

Imagination

WHY DID I COVER YOUR HEAD IN GOLDEN tresses or with dark, luscious curls? Because I am the God of cascades and waterfalls, of tumbling fire and waves falling over themselves to roll onto shore or over your precious pates. For what lies inside your head is my treasure trove, deep wells of imagination and the ability to be in awe of my creation and my loving hand. The means to wonder at the wondrous and ponder things, here and in your hearts.

A mind that belongs to me is special indeed, and its synapses sparkle with my Spirit going to and fro, sending ideas back and forth of things unseen, yet fashioned out of filament and daydreams.

What happens in heads not filled with selfish sugar plums is a constant source of delight to me and my servant host. The thoughts and tales that come! The pictures that travel there! The rhymes that arrive! This is a reflection of my infinite capabilities, echoed in you within the complexities of language, thought, and colour.

In such a head, all sacred in origin, anything is possible. A myriad of new worlds is just rustling behind the curtain of your imaginations, waiting to be discovered, waiting excitedly to break through.

Selah

Clocks

*T*IME IS NOT YOURS TO WORRY OVER, to fret about or to number. This life is not for clock watching, but clock-making. You and I make the gears together, we fit their movements and wind them. We use them as guides, not tyrants.

Time was not invented to dominate us, but to help us pray the hours, to divide out the days and balance each portion so that no duty became too heavy, nor our souls depleted for lack of sleep and play.

Don't kill time, this gift that was given, nor kowtow to it, as if it were some unwelcome monstrous houseguest, maliciously ticking and eating away your life from the corner of the room. No, this is not the way!

Roll with the movement, like a child rolls down a grassy bank. Tick along with the seasons, like a meadow knows when to lift a poppy's head, or nest a field mouse, when to lie fallow and draw up goodness from the ground, and when to send it back.

Learn the flow, the ebb, and the tides of the beginning, the middle, and the end. Savour the moments and fear not the swift passing of joy or the ending of laughter's visits, paid all too fleetingly.

You did not miss anything, you lived. Nothing is passing you by, you are here. Smile, relax, and let my time settle into your bones, as more of it trickles under your feet like a cool stream.

Do not rush at time, like a cornered beast; lie on your back and let it tickle your upturned belly, for time is a playmate, a helper, a slackened rule, galactic material playing and twisting around your fingers. It bends to my will even as it holds your days together and runs up the seam between your days and your nights. Love it, luxuriate in it—it is a holy servant.

Selah

Topsy-Turvy

*T*HE WORLD IS FULL OF CONTRADICTIONS and paradoxes. The closing of eyes which enables us to see clearly for the first time. The leaf that dies to bring new life to the soil, taking sunshine from the tips of branches to the base of the tree that bore it.

The process began in the garden where the choosing of the knowledge of good and evil was itself the first sin, the desire to know and the desire to do ever intermingled.

How to learn from this and go forward, my children? By going backwards, falling down and coming back up again by presenting yourselves helpless (as you are) before me. Strength comes by weakness, a road barely travelled but which will continue to save and heal all peoples with the wisdom of its weary nomads.

And where two or more travel this dusty road together, learning from hearing my voice at their shoulders, this too will feed the world, which came also from dust. My breath in you will return to its owner, to its source, and you with it. And those who have sated themselves on lack, on pain and suffering, will feed the rest of my lambs. This is my "upside down" way, which sets things the right way up, and which nearly all humankind eschews, but which is the nectar of this living, breathing, loving God.

Selah

Gem

A DIAMOND NEED NOT FEAR A CHAINSAW. It is too unwieldy and barbaric an instrument to cut her. And even the tools that can splinter such a gem, which would be made from titanium or from its own cousins, need not be feared, for what is to be lost by being spliced or given more facets?

Even if she were to fragment into a million shining pieces, each one would be as beautiful as the first and more light would be spread abroad in the world. So a jewel like this, true to itself and formed under great pressure in the depths, need fear no-one and no-thing, for man truly can do nothing to harm her.

All who see her are astounded at her beauty and the glory-light she refracts in every heavenly hue. A true diamond knows that her admirers love her for the grace she carries, the light she reflects, the hope she embodies, of light being mined from the darkness, and of beauty born of burdens.

Selah

Chamber of Secrets

*T*HE CHAMBER OF SECRETS IS A PLACE, not of hiding, but of revelation, and it exists within your heart. It is the place where all your dreams and treasures lie, unguarded and waiting, aching to be discovered. They were set there, falling from my fingertips like blessed rain after drought, and sit ready to make all things green again.

Yes, your heart too may be made new, bursting forth in leaf and bud, my holy *viriditas* verdancy of greening, groaning with the desire to be unleashed upon your dry, cracked heart. Let it all pour forth in a voyage of blessing and uncovering. Let it show the way, guiding you between rocks and to all the islands of your own personal odyssey. For I alone know the path you must take and I hold the wheel and the rudder of your life.

Let the rushing of living water, poured from my clouded breath, form oceans around you. Look into the clear surface and see the secrets made visible, your face in mine, my heart in yours, and togetherness only hitherto dreamed of in your wildest attempts to apprehend my Grace and Goodness.

All is here, ready to flow, ready to be released. Find the chamber of my heart locked inside yours, and let its waters roar!

Selah

Porthole

YOU CAN LOOK AT THE DEEPEST OCEAN through the safety of a porthole, but all you will see is a misted impression, muddied by your own reflection and soiled by spots of cabin lighting. To truly see the ocean, one must open wide the way and swim out into seeming darkness, bold and unafraid.

Here you will find your way, lit by coral torches and signposted by fronds of kelp, reaching banner-like to the surface. Hold on, stop and stare, marvel at the strangeness of creatures you never thought to see in this life or in any other! Be amazed at the variety of the ocean's bounty and find your lungs filled with songs of praise, rising then in magical bubbles to burst into music on reaching the world above.

Here there are so many wonders that you will struggle to name them all, finding the waters thick with new life. Teeming depths are here for you to explore and enjoy, a never-ending pilgrimage of joy, taking far more than 20,000 leagues to traverse! And all this, that you glimpse now, in your imagination, is but a scratching on the edge of a rock in the side of a planet, for like your Hubble telescope that tantalizes with pictures of my handiwork, so these depths are only a taste of what is to come. And even this tiny fraction of bounty will set your heart fit to burst in soaring awe.

Speak then to those who think my kingdom boring, or who think heaven will be a school assembly where they are doomed to ever long for playtime. No! This is life in abundance, and it will satisfy all your longings. There are more colours here than you could dream up, and more beauty than your soul needs to sup on for all eternity! You gaze through your dull porthole if you must, but see enough to make you want to dive in!

Selah

Rainbow

*T*HIS GENTLE DRIZZLE PITTER-PATTERING on the roof is nothing compared to the deluge of love that is to come—the torrent of wisdom words and the downpour roaring of rainbow colours—for my promise itself, the whole spectrum of hues, shall be the thing that next floods the world.

Waterfalls of sparkling beauty, tints of every kind, named and unnamed, glinting in the rush of living water. The crashing, roaring excitement of heaven pouring out her heart onto the rocks below, crashing down on your unworthy beloved heads, imaginations fuelled by the glimpsing of distant galaxies and unknown stars as they circle and shine here in the pool of my reflections, gathered calmly here below, where still waters run deep.

Let the colours come! Let the colours come here in your eyes, your heart, your mind, let them play, let them dance! And bring forth for me a cascade of joyful laughter in recognition of the first six days of ART, and let me say, this too is very good!

Selah

Tears

*T*HE LEVEL IN THE WELL OF DISCONTENT RISES with every deluge; self-pity streams its way in through underground channels when we are not looking or choosing to look the other way. Poison seeps in from jealous looks and determinations to only see one side of things; the green damp on the brickwork is rotten and climbing.

The water here is stale and stagnant, for the incoming springs are lazy and have no life in them. Their very molecules clutch life to their selfish chests, not letting any escape, holding everything so tightly that it is of as much use and comfort as a miser's gold, hoarded and invisible, all energy spent on not spending. And the water rises, unclean and clenched to its own good.

No freshness is poured out here, nor will the goodness of a single drop be drunk, for nothing is given, nothing is open, all is closed and sneering, like an old man living in fear of death instead of being freed by joy. Change is feared, transformation avoided. The darkness suits the dank water as the levels rise.

One drop, one drop only of release, of open-hearted sweetness, gifted into this gloomy tunnel, would cause a ripple of clarity, an opening of the well of the soul, a chain reaction. One tear cried in happy, selfless abandon for another, one beautiful, caring salted droplet, would freshen this deathly water and bring cleansing of the slimy walls, and a tide of tears that would push out the poison and unclench the holding fists. Waves of change would come, and the well would be healed.

Never hold to yourself what may be released. Set the captives free, yes, even the tears you have held inside all these years, and let them join the flow of my love as it surges along and changes the chemical composition of all the world's waterways.

Selah

Smoke

MOKE SIGNALS RISE HIGH ABOVE THE ROOFTOPS and the towers. Signs of the burning in people's hearts, but not for me. How I long for their desiring minds and grasping emotions to turn full face to me, but they will not. They dream of lottery wins and fast cars and of the glory and approval of the camera, which always lies and pays its minions well.

How shall I compete with these trifles? I will not. I have no need to. I am above all this, and yet my heart cries out even as I sit beside them on the sofa or weep with longing by the screens they pour their time and energy into. I stand by the frantically waving stockbrokers, and the purring, sated fat cats as they wine and dine a new client, all the time winking at one another, their whiskers bristling, sizing up their prey.

Their self-congratulatory stomachs so full of food that was never theirs to take sicken me. But still I am there, waiting, hoping to catch their eye, to spark a light, to send a dart of hope and alternative, of the possibility of true love, shooting down a cortex or through a vein. But all is clogged with the cholesterol of cash, and the vision misted by a cloud of self so sure of that self and nothing else.

And the poor too, once my people, shun me. They dine on pretence and hold the copper coins out in their palms, not to place in the poor box, but to drop in the fat cats' many hats—to fuel the illusion and the fears, caught in a consumer all-is-greener-brighter-over-here trap. And the emotions and the hunger that roar in them and should be mine become only a confusing painful noise that must be sent to sleep at all costs, not seen and not heard, punched, drunk, drugged, comatose, lobotomized by the torrent of cheap images and fast food.

Ah, but I still will sit there, and gaze at all of them with love. For I am the everlasting love that they yearn for, not so deep down, and some will reach, and some will see, and some will ask, and some will run home to me, and together we can build a new world, outside these walls, where the smoke that rises is from loving hearts and those who come home, and are sat around my campfires, telling their tales and keeping one another warm.

Selah

Tremors

*T*REMORS ARE SIGNS, NOT OF WEAKNESS, but of building strength. They will cause mountains to rise from the earth, even as men's towers fall. Things that quake and crumble come, not before their time, but to build upon the foundations of a crumbled world. Those broken bricks and bones will hold strongly underneath my temple, death becoming life and resurrection. For all is being made anew and you shall see it before your very eyes, aflame with delight and wonder, this remaking of all things.

Time begets nothing but more time, and these then produce haste and misery. Let us then stop measuring days and nights and begin afresh a world without time, a place formed from dreams and mists, a kingdom born of mystery and awe. A planet that does not need to be held down by guide ropes or explained by laws, but whose very existence is come from music, from the crystal laughter of singing souls, the joy of soaring birds—a place birthed from the colours in the fire and the diamond. A defying of limits, of the boundaries of imagination, and a realizing of everything good and true, wise and beautiful. Let the world shake and be turned inside out! Let the newness come!

Selah

Oases

*E*ACH POOL YOU REACH IS A BREAK FOR A SANITY check. A remembering that depths sustain you and run underneath all you are and do. A place to close eyes, lift up made-holy-by-encounter hands and a voice trained to listen. Stop, pause, breathe; be restored, recalibrated to the richness held in silence and stillness, but do not imagine that you yet belong here, or that you can stay. For if you tarry too long the flames that surround the pool will lap you up and singe your edges. This other world is coming, but it is not yet.

Taste and move on: perpetual transition, the propelling dance of love and life, is your element for the present. Linger in my love, do, and stop to show me your heart, heaving with heavenly longings, but then smile, take a deep breath, and continue with your worldly work, for it was set before you for many reasons.

I need you as a signpost for the lost, a tavern for the weary, a dancer for the joyless and a beacon for the wandering hordes, showing the way to the hopeless, shining my light on the path. For if you too stop and keep watch with me, who then will find my lambs and speak my heart to them?

Again, I say this is not yet. Now is working your way, river to ocean, life to life through death, your face beaming with the knowing of me that comes from dancing the dance, walking the walk, letting the waves roll you along the shore. Be fluid, carried by tides then, secure in the knowledge that your destination is held safe in my hands, awaiting your heart at the end of the journey.

Selah

Swims

*E*ACH PERSON HAS THEIR OWN SWIM. They may go awry and beyond the ropes now and again, but when they do, they feel it, and the world seems wrong, like an ill-fitting suit. You were each built for a particular swim, so stick to it. Do not try to cross lanes or stop others in their tracks, asking stupid questions about how to be them. You can only be yourself. That is who you are and why you were made, to be perfectly you. Do that then, with my help.

Learn the stroke that is comfortable, not easy, but the one with which you can travel along and not be foiled by cramp, the one that fits in with the way you breathe; for so much of life, including the spiritual, is about rhythm, about timings, about the tide of breathing in and out. Do not imagine this is ordinary, for all breath is holy and sacred, and so should the words be that coast along on it, and the emotions that are let out on it.

Swim then, my dearest children, and not in competition with anyone, not the person next to you or with yourself, and certainly not with me. Swim surely and safely, take time to breathe and lift your head and look around, but do not think you can be still for too long, or you will sink. Life goes on, and you are all on a journey along the rivers to the heart of my ocean, or the ocean of my heart, and all of you are finding your way home, to your birthing place, leaping hurdles to reach me, and many weary miles of endurance will carry you here to where you belong. I am waiting here with open arms even as I glide alongside you, ears and heart open, all the time. Minnow or whale, sprat or ancient leviathan, I am your constant companion and guide on the waterways.

Selah

Work and Play

*T*HE WORLD IS A NUISANCE TO YOU AND YET is also my beloved, like a little sister who demands attention, to be played with and adored. You feel tortuously pulled, as though the draughty silence of cobwebbed rooms were where I wanted you, and not here, laughing with the little and the small.

Spin tops and turn tables, feel the freedom of the young and the unmanned—the child must run free, fast and footloose, shrieking till the breath is laboured, giggling through the chase and the thrills of swinging high and spinning round. Play is just as holy as work, squealing gales of laughter just as sacred as breezes of quiet contemplation. Do not judge between them or imagine some part of your life, your day, your home, more holy than others—all is mine, all is enveloped in life and love.

The only time I frown is when you turn your face away. Be mine always in everything, smile inside if joy cannot reach your face, leap and bound in your imagination if your limbs feel lifeless. In every thought come running to me and fling your school sandals into the hedgerows where they belong!

Selah

Bruises

*T*ONGUES ARE SHARP, like the winter air ripe with the potential to freeze, and the wounds they inflict are like frostbite—black and unhealable. But my words are soft and sure, low and easy, a balm to your soul. Even where they pinch a little, it is a nudging reminder of the curb, where and how far you have strayed, a setting straight.

All is healing, of fractured ways and lost souls and the bruises from the past that still have the power to bloom and colour today's skin. I can soothe them and help you muster the spiritual strength and salve to persuade them to fade. With me your skin can be perfect again, not because the surface is smoothed over or covered with concealer, but because the hurting places underneath are transformed by my healing grace.

Selah

Hell

*T*HERE IS A WEEPING AND GNASHING OF TEETH in every heart that beats. For hell is the broken places, the grief-stricken paralysis, the cold numb terror, the fear that overrides hope, the rising bile that sweeps all kind tides out of its path and surges on regardless of anyone else's feelings. But inside each hellish torment is the help of angels, if you will only call upon it.

Each fear may be named and tamed, each deluge of poison drained away into holy gutters where sanctification may take place and all waters run clear again.

Do not be afraid of these words that seem fearless and harsh, too strong for human ears, for they are here to help and do no harm, they are come as a silver-traced balm made from hidden herbs deep in heaven's forest glades, where the moon's beams are harnessed and turned into petals, crushed to make a liniment of light.

Darkness is never the whole story, and while clouds are not lined with precious metal, the rain that falls carries the freshness of dew ready to cloak in softness or remedy all things.

Be glad, therefore, of the showers that fall and the sanctuaries that beat bright and cheerful in the chambers of your heart, for they shall not be silenced. Flow will always beat stagnation, and my holy warm breath will cure petrification wherever it occurs, no matter how deep or sulphurous the cavern, or how deadly the poisoned dart.

Selah

Repetition

D O NOT BE AFRAID TO REPEAT YOURSELVES. Do not be afraid to go over and over the same ground, for this is how we strengthen things, like the vines that lash logs together to make a raft. How shall it float free if the vines do not go back and forth, closing round and back on themselves many times?

Do not imagine that everything that is said or written or made must be all newness, for there is no such thing. We only say the same thing in new ways, in hopes of gaining insight and understanding.

As people who create ways to speak my truth, you are bound only to be faithful to the Way, the Truth, and the Life, and not to innovation or trends. My words and wishes will always stand the test of time, and my living water never grows tired or stale. Serve it up then, in new vessels if you wish, but remember that I am never boring, lacklustre, or tedious, and even if I say the same thing many times over, my love is never dull!

Selah

Brow

*O*N THE BROW OF THE VERY STEEP HILL there is a moment where you choose. You choose either fear or hope as you stand transfixed by the incline of the slope. It is a time to decide whenever you will roll down, rough and tumble, embracing the grass and sheep pellets and goose-grass footballs that will inevitably attach themselves to you; or if you will pussyfoot, tentative toeholds, rolling back on your heels in terror and an attempt to dig in.

Can you throw yourself into it, this life? Or will you encase the brittleness of your bones in prodigious care that leaves no room for fun or rolling, breathless laughter?

And what choice shall you make on the brow of your sight, poised to look at the world through the poverty of your frowning lens? Shall fear or joy win the day? You can give yourself entirely over to fretful tears or let my peace rule, both in your heart and in the eyes of your heart.

Yes, bad things might happen, you could break a limb. But sister death awaits at the bottom of the rolling in any case for everyone. The only question is whether you arrive there in a gasping, giggling heap, full of life and spinning with wonder, or on fearful tiptoes, having never felt the scratch of a thorn.

Selah

Teaspoons

*T*EASPOONS ARE MADE TO HOLD SMALL AMOUNTS. They are for grains of sugar and drizzling honey. They are given small tasks. If you want to dig a tunnel for a motorway, you do not bring teaspoons. Yet some of you who are teaspoons gaze longingly at the motorway workers, with their diggers and pneumatic drills, and think, I wish I could do that, instead of the work of making tea and soothing throats and giving medicine.

I wonder, my loves, how many more spiritual superhighways need to be built before you see them for the nonsense they are. For I am the God of the tiny and the lost, the God who will meet you in the sympathy and sweetness of a hot drink stirred with love, not on the stage of a megachurch or in a millionaire's mantra.

I will sing to you softly in the dark and curl up alongside you in the sobbing, silent hours. I am where two or three meet together, with listening hearts and eyes glistening with tenderness, not in the sharpness of white teeth and the game-show-host dais.

Sit with one another then, and stir grains of love into your honeyed tea, and do not concern yourselves with what is larger, what is shinier, what is "greater." For my comfort is all here before you, in tannin-stained metal and chipped china, in warming wonder and the giving of togetherness.

Selah

The Faceless Saint

*F*AME IS GIVEN THE SLIP, and her followers are few, pushing the cart on which she slowly travels wheellessly under no power known to this earth. More often than not, stuck in the mud, waiting. She lifts her head in constancy to the Lord, but history has recorded no face to remember, no name to call her by. She lived a small and unnatural life, holy as hell-driven-out in every molecule of her heart for him, and struck only ever by the Lord's lightning, she burnt with zeal and sacred flame.

The only place she desires remembrance is in the solid chambers of his heart. The rooms untethered to anything but him, always pulled by cords invisible, binding her to his love. Prayer her only virtue, her only goal, her only gift.

She will hold your hand silently, but you will not know it. She will lift your heart along with her own to the Lord, but never know the credit for it. She will pour out her love on his altar for those she has never met, not resorting to words.

No-one can truly love me without also loving my children, whether they ever know for whom they weep and pray. Thus a hermit may effect more good in the world than an entire battalion of angels. These are secret things, and it is not your task to judge or count, only to trust. Once I am loved, all are loved.

Selah

Noticing

*T*AKE THE TIME TO NOTICE. That is what so few do. Not when reading the Scriptures, not in relationship, not in listening prayer. What needs to be noticed? What is crying out to be heard? What is sitting up begging to be taken notice of? What is stretching its hand to the ceiling in desperate eagerness to answer your question and so keen for you to say, "Yes, you!" that it is scraping the tiptoes of its schoolgirl shoes across the linoleum floor out of sight under the desk? The angst of waiting for you to notice is unbearable.

Can you notice the tell-tale signs? The unmended rip, the despondency as the laugh tails off, the solid obstinacy of the grin, the pain of too many unsaid "*I love you*'s" behind the tired eyes, the cringing from not being touched, the screaming shell of ego wrapped around the tiniest nut of true self? Can we now stop pretending that everything is fine and start noticing these things about one another? Can we let our pain then speak and when someone asks how we are, tell them? Can we listen to the real answers, even when they are unspoken? Can we lean in to them with love?

Can we learn to stop and home in on the tells? Because choosing not to is like walking past on the other side. And while we cannot do this for everyone on the planet, can we do it for ourselves and those who have been entrusted to our love? Can we give and receive noticing, and then learn to respond with grace, time, and understanding?

Some cries for help are less audible than others, and sometimes that faint aroma of sweetness on the edge of your senses is the crushed bud of someone's hope or dream, being kicked about underfoot, trampled on in the playground, the road, the supermarket, the kitchen. Your floors are littered with the corpses of dreams, faded and lost. Could you be one of those who gather them, tenderly and with real tears? Could you create a beautiful fragrance out of them? Could they be made into the notes of a new perfume, one fit to rise before God? Could you be a perfumier of prayer? That the lost ones, the broken ones, might be released before the throne of heaven, so that all those desperate hopes that never found their way might now be brought home?

Such things are the work of God's people.

Selah

Absolutes and Burdens

*T*HERE ARE NO CERTAINTIES. Even things you think you know, like my goodness, reach far beyond your vision, extending, drawing back from your ability to apprehend like the edges of the sea, drawing out for mile upon endless mile. You cannot know these or any other things with totality, you can only make shrewd or heart-led guesses, estimates that fall deliciously and laughably short of the mark.

Not that your lack of understanding amuses me, my dearest, but that it is sweet to me, as you try to comprehend, like a mother watching her child try to master its first words, or a master indeed watching a puppy first try to run and keep up. For you could not come to heel if I walked at my speed; I must slow to yours. And I do this out of love, a deep and expressive compassion that knows no bounds that you would be able to grasp.

And so, we begin speaking, by teaching you consonants, and sibilants, and you take the learning on board and imagine you can speak with angels. And so you shall. But not yet, and not soon, for there is such a long way to go. Isn't it so much easier and lighter to write my words rather than your own? Isn't laboriousness tiresome? And yet you will stick to your duty and your ethic of deserving, your trying and striving to do better. This is not the way.

Lean in to me and not on your own understanding. Fall deeper through my skin and flesh of my flesh till you reach the inner courts and the heart of me.

Here you will find pools of delicious, tantalizingly clear water that reflects and holds everything good and whole. This is the well I want you to drink from and leave that bitter cup of effort behind. Then you will not be able to say, "I did this," but only, "I found this, buried deep in the heart of God." And the glory belongs, then, in its rightful place. For the bondservant of love does not say of the master, "I served him well today, did I not?" but rather, "I wish I could serve him better," and this is how to do it, not looking to your own talents and prowess, but to the goal of pleasing me.

As for me, I look to have you close, and to remove these frightful burdens, these rocks you roll around each day as though they might bring forth living water or conceal hidden treasure that might be released by pushing them up hills.

My darling child, say yes, and come into my sanctuary, and be set free from this yoke you imagine is your destiny. Let me help you set it down and break it into the dust. I am your home, come to me. Come home to me, and dance.

Selah

Still, Small Voice

*T*HOUGH YOU TRY TO DEADEN THE STILL, small voice it will come unbidden in the night, a shaft of light in the darkness, a soft sweet singing in the pause between appointments. Gently insistent, it will be seen and heard. And then, how foolish your lives will seem!

Like a gardener watching and waiting for a compost heap to bear apples with her back turned to an orchard as vast as the sky. Like an astronomer hell-bent on searching space for a star to name after himself, when I have painted a whole galaxy for him to call home.

Before you waste one more second on pointless endeavours, hold still, and hear the poetry of your own heartbeat. Listen for the words that are rolling unsaid around your speech like waves of curling grace. These are the spaces that cannot help but fill with the presence of God.

If you each knew your worth to me or had tasted one drop of the ocean of my mighty and fearsome love, you would tremble and laugh at the smallness of your vision and your tiny, tinny hearts I hold so dear.

Selah

Thieves

*T*HE LITTLE FOX-JACKALS COME, and they wind their tails around the vines beguilingly. They devour the grapes behind your back and grin at you later with wide charm. A glint of sharpness and a flash of red or brown fur, and they are gone, leaving you scratching your chin and wondering how you ever let them into the vineyard.

Do not fret about these bounders, nor about any nighttime burglars or daylight thieves, for the Lord gives such bounty as to be endlessly more-than-enough, and so you may give and be taken from cheerfully. Do not spend your energy batting away every fly, or you will never eat!

My abundance is there for all and makes no sense to those still playing by the rules of the world. They are like orphans who steal apples from the king's orchard, never dreaming that they are all adopted royalty and may waltz in and eat their fill whenever they like.

Laugh, therefore, when someone takes from you, for it shall be given back to you tenfold, and all that will have happened is that you helped to feed one of my own.

Selah

Milestones

Y OU LEAVE MARKERS ALONG THE WAY. Big birthdays, new jobs, anniversaries of joy and disaster. Yet these are not the remembrance stones I set up or write down in my book of life.

For me, your significant moments are less about measuring and more about when your heart says yes to me. Even then, a deeper joy than the altar call or the baptism comes from that instant when you were lost in the dark, forlorn of hope, and yet still cried out to me, knowing I would not forsake you, believing I had not left you to face the pain alone, even though everyone and the world told you that I had.

That moment you insisted on my goodness, in the midst of the fog, at the bottom of the ocean with your head wrapped in seaweed, or in the desert wanderings, when still you held faith that clarity would come, that a whale was on its way, that water might spring forth from a rock at any moment. These are my treasured memories of you, and they are marked forever in my heart.

Selah

Butter

ID YOU KNOW THAT BUTTER SINGS? That yellow-gold sounds like trumpets and that I see the bell of a cornet when its praises rise up to me? For all the world is burgeoning with the knowledge of my goodness, and the music is curling up to me from everywhere in sweet, melodious aromas.

Churned and beaten, then patted into shape, was ever milk so violently treated? And might it not have every seeming right to stay cold and rigid, holding to its shape and hardness as the one thing left of its own? But even as it suffers, it knows that its colour and taste are its glory, and that they would not be without the dairywoman's rolled-up sleeves and wooden paddles.

Singing out as it cannot help but do, it melts, and releases all the goodness it has been given to contain. Is it not the same for every created thing? Pain will be redeemed in glory, and songs cannot help but escape the misery and rise heartfelt, harmonious before my throne.

Selah

Serenity

*T*ROUBLED THOUGHTS ASSAIL YOU. They stir in your heart from time to time, and swirl in your stomach. They growl and they flutter, bringing unrequested turbulence.

Do not fear these sensations, but instead ask for and receive my sweet woodland peace, so that, like a shaft of light coming upon you suddenly as you round a dark corner, or the unhurried arias of a nearby robin, hopping from branch to branch to be near you as you stumble forward, all worries will be silenced by soothing awe.

This Edenic clearing is at the centre of all thing, it contains soul serenity, a deep and ancient "magic" known to saints and storytellers throughout the ages, and there is a wellspring here that runs clear and sure.

Come here often, and slake your thirst, drinking with eyes closed and heart open, knowing the sacred touch of the love that binds all things together. This is my serenity spring, and it will sustain the peace, the balance in you, when all the world seems noisy and chaotic. When life disturbs and distresses you, come here to taste and remember that the truth is all love and goodness. This centre will always hold.

And it will move out in ever-widening ripples of calm delight.

Selah

Rollercoaster

I PUT YOU ON THE ROLLERCOASTER NOW AND AGAIN, even though some of you hate it. At first it seems as though this is a malicious act, the whim of an uncaring parent. But it is not that.

For how will you traverse mountain ranges later, if I do not teach you about highs and lows now? How will you sail through galaxies, laughing into solar winds, if you do not learn how to take unexpected bends now? White knuckles are part of the ride, just as much as calm meanderings.

The landscape of love must rise and fall, or else the deserts will encroach on farmland, and the oceans will have no boundaries or depths to contain them. Learn to trust your maker and, since there is nothing else to be done, go with the flow. All your control is illusory and the motion unstoppable. There will be time enough later for the gentleness and sweet music of the carousel and the Ferris wheel, for their circles are always turning. You are not missing out, but here and now on this ride, trust me, and have the time of your life.

Selah

Fireball

*T*HERE IS A CORE OF TRUTH, a sphere of fire in your belly. When the rest of you is quieted, you can feel it slowly turning, aflame with deep peace and knowing. This is the part of you that holds firm to what is right and good and true, to me.

When you pray or listen with compassion, it roars into life and infuses everything with the quiet passion of Christ. When you deny it and try to hide from me, or utter soulless, selfish desires masquerading as prayers, when your heart is not in your words, it fades and becomes dull and lifeless, dormant, waiting for the arousal of compassion which is its oxygen.

It is not something you can always feel, but you know it lives in you, for when you begin to traverse and explore God you begin to delve deeper also into your own self, and to sit with the places where you reflect his loving glory and unfathomable kindness, along with his gracious wisdom.

Fireballs and flames can crackle fiercely, but they can also burn gently and be full of soft colours and subtle sighs. Fire, too, can flow. Let it hold the centre and run through your veins—into the sparkle of your eyes whenever you speak *of* me, and the warmth of your smile whenever you speak *with* me.

Selah

Petals

*B*LOSSOMS ARE MORE BEAUTIFUL, petals prettier, when they let the light shine through. The light comes streaming from behind them, and they cannot see it, or know it is there, but they are sure it is not at them alone others are gazing in wonder.

Such are my people, who let my light come through and shine in ways they themselves cannot see. I know how best to illuminate my own creation, how to show off its delicate colours and seep through its translucent frailty, how to make it glow with heavenly delight.

Trust me then, to have made you perfectly for the light that will reach out to the world through the thin and wearing patches of you that feel the least holy. Trust me to shine out of the cracks and woundings, through the gaps you are desperate to fill. These may be the very places you join with me in shining bright.

Do not, then, be in such a hurry to "fix" yourselves or to cover yourselves in heavy layers of protection, for it may be that to others, your fragility is precisely where my glory meets and awes the world. And this too is wholeness.

Selah

Mussels

*B*LACK AND BARNACLED, trailing aged seaweed beards, some of you will stick to anything. You will take your place on an idea or a translation and park yourself there for what you imagine to be eternity. There will be no shifting you; however arbitrary the beginning of the glue, it will remain your footing for everything you ponder.

Is it wise to invest all you are told now with such childish roots and thoughts? Each and every time the tide comes in to wash you away you refuse to budge, holding yourself so tightly shut that no living water can persuade you of the size or wonder in the ocean. When the stillness and the air come back, or the shallowness returns you to comfort, you sigh and stroke your shell and chatter amongst those who sit stuck with you.

Do you not know you are doing things the wrong way around? For it is when the water is over your head that you should be feeding, filtering the morsels from the brine. And when you are above the ebb and flow, you should clamp your lips shut and not speak of the wonders you have seen until you have digested them fully.

And I say, it is good to become unglued and travel the swiftness of currents! I say, it is good to look at the vastness of the seas from a vantage point less stultified. To examine another view, to imagine, maybe, what it might be like not to be a mussel, always exercising your own strength and sticking power, and instead, learning to swim by watching dolphins, or to sing by listening to whales. Good to consider the billions of lives surrounding you, feeding you, living in deep and different waters, telling you of places you have never been and filling your small head with shell-shattering ideas!

Relax, let go, come with me, and learn about the flow of freedom, the liberty of love.

Selah

Daffodils

*D*OES A DAFFODIL LONG TO BE a different colour? Anything other than the same glorious yellow trumpeting against a deep blue sky? Never, for it trusts the wisdom and the heart that painted it, and it is only we who seek to create hybrids and other palettes for each of God's creations.

Does the fanfare that brasses out of its golden bell wish it were a different tune? Does it long to whisper soft flutings across the flower bed? No, because it trusts the song it was given, and gladly gives it voice.

How much more, then, should you stop seeking to change or embellish your own God-given tasks and beauty, and just give your all to the you who is already present! Sing her song, lift his voice, let them bloom and dazzle and be. For just as nothing but pillars of pure sunshine will do as a herald of blue skies and springtime, so your soul is made exactly as it was intended, and your song lies within you intact and raring to be released into the world.

Selah

Stretching

ON'T BE ALARMED OR DISCOURAGED, my darlings, if I ask you questions and urge you to think. For all of this is done under my auspices and in the safe sanctuary of my courts. I am only prompting you to travel deeper, to know better, to become more, to find yourselves in me, and me in yourselves.

For what greater adventure is there than to make your way into wider, more spacious places, full of my life and love? To learn and discover more of your own souls, which live and move and breathe in the vastness of me, the One who loves?

Rejoice, then, in the passing of all time spent doing soul work, whether at my feet or in my arms, learning and loving, pruning earth to help heaven bloom.

For if I do not challenge you now, here in your smallness, to wonder and ponder greater things, how shall you ever set foot on heaven's driveway? First steps can feel strangely unbalanced, but I am here, reaching out to you, to my darlings, as you learn to walk in my ways, and I will always pick you up with a proud, loving smile when you stumble. Follow the sound of my voice, and with your heart, mind, and soul keep on making your way home.

Selah

Washing Line

*I*MAGINE ALL THE CLOTHES YOU HAVE EVER WORN are pegged out along a washing line. From diapers to blue jeans, workaday denim on the same plane as midnight satin, the little black dress and the long white wedding gown, all part of the one long stream of your life.

Does any of it define you, my love? Does your taste or your size or do the labels ever amount to more than shells, casings that you grew out of like a hermit crab, crawling into the next thing for a while? Could you hang the names people have given you here too? Daughter, child, sister, brother, girlfriend, wife, lover, mother, son, aunt, cousin, friend, loser, liberal, cleaner, writer, patient, deadbeat, heartbreaker, fool. Suppose these too are just pegged labels, swinging in the drying breeze, and do not define your wholeness either.

What then? Who might you be, if not these things, outer and relational? What name might you call yourself, or might you answer to? Or instead of the name, is it the right voice to which you will bend your ear now and allow to call you by a secret moniker, written on white stone, pressed into your palm by holy love?

Can you cast off all these linear, temporal hangings, and laugh joyfully as your bare feet touch the grass below, pegs flying this way and that as you run to me, calling your forever name, that means (and will ever mean) Beloved? Come away then, arise, and come away with me!

Selah

Shape

$\mathcal{L}$ OOK CLOSELY AT YOUR SKIN and you will find it full of grooves. This smoothness you are in constant search of is illusory, a fake front, like so many facades the world chases after. Instead, remember that each of your precious fingers bears a grain, like the bark and heartwood of trees. Under a microscope you would see furrows, streams of flesh running into one another, like tributaries to the river of life.

Go further still and you would be astonished to find you are made of molecules with boundless space between them. Finally, it would become clear to you that even your shape is temporal, constantly flowing in and out of its own edges, back and forth beyond your perceived reality, dancing tidally through life.

For soon you may come to understand that you too are a universe expanding, taking in and becoming more and more of the life around you, reaching out as you breathe, for more and more of love to reform you. Soon you may see that it is all through life and not just in the womb that you are knitted together by your creator, remade perfection over and over again until your flesh is worn so thin and is so transparent with light that it is time to step out of one shape and into another. Something which should not scare you, my loves, since you have been practicing for this all your lives.

Selah

Beginnings

*E*VERYTHING BEGINS. It begins with a spark, a dot, or a seed. One small mark on a blank piece of paper. Even universes have their beginnings, in laughs that rise up from my belly, and then burst out into blooms of flowering creation.

Be mindful, then, of what you begin and how you start. Once something commences, it can be hard to stop. Even the smallest results started a long time before, set in motion by the longings of your heart or the machinations of your mind, or the conniving of your ego.

Learn to discern, then, a good beginning from a bad one, and your burgeoning crop will never need to be burnt down or replaced, nor shall it yield a lukewarm, bland grain, good for nothing and devoid of nutrients.

In the spring, look over your seeds with me; let us pray together, examining motive and desire, plans and possibilities, before we plant them. In the winter, let us make the snowball from a collection of perfect crystals before we roll it over the crisp white ground. For make no mistake, it may gather to a great size and become unstoppable as it carries itself onwards, and many have unwittingly started avalanches this way.

Ask for all things to have their genesis in me, and pray my will be done, and then we can partner in creative joy and maybe watch another galaxy burst into flower!

Selah

Beyond

$\mathcal{M}$Y DARLING, DO YOU KNOW THAT BEYOND this world is another, full of hope? That what you feel now, this slow and deliberate devouring of your life, is playing right into my hands, and that this is exactly where you want and need it to be? For this other world is just a finger's breadth, a heartbeat, a soft sigh away.

We can travel there any instant you choose, so that you may taste the sweetness of the source of your faith and feel the brine in the air from the currents of Spirit that dance there in my oceans, performing ballet after ballet of love.

What divides you from this place is a laughable sliver, and you *will* laugh one day when you come home. For now, it remains a joyful wonder you can only hint at, only glimpse, only snatch a tantalizing whiff of, as though it were an unattainable heavenly apple pie, sitting on a ledge way out of reach. But at the same time as you long for it, you gain more than a sneak preview. Each time you cross the threshold, even for a moment, you are more solidly anchored to your real home, which is why those who devote themselves to prayer are always homesick.

And one day, when this is more real to you than your earthly abode, here will become there and there will be no more straining to hear the song, no more closing your eyes tighter to see better, no more cricking of your neck to see beyond the cleft of rock to catch a glimpse of my glory.

For on that day I shall bring you home and our joy shall be unsurpassed.

Selah

Ash

*T*HE FLAKES DRIFT DOWN ONTO YOUR SLEEPING form, and watching from outside the dream, you cannot understand why they do not wake you, for they are white hot as if fresh from a holy volcano of Spirit. All they do is burst into flame upon touching you, as though your skin were even more scorching. The pale ash is consumed, and you are surrounded by an aura of burning brightness.

Holy, holy, holy is the Lord God Almighty, maker of heaven and earth, and the earth is full of his glory, evident here upon the softly smiling lips and the weeping lashes, leaking sweet tears only released when you dream-walk upon lands otherwise unknown.

Somewhere else entirely, you wander barefoot in green gardens, and despite the fiery reality, all feels lushly cool. Is this summer evening on another plane, or is this the depth that underlies earthly happenings? What level of being has claimed you here, where your head turns at the raucous cry of the phoenix in the trees, rising from the ruins of who you once were?

You are covered in the glorious mantle of God's love, sleeping and waking, and everything of him longs to rain down and settle upon you, to touch the one who is so beloved. So comes the ash, and the snow, the rain and the blossom, to begin above and end below, festooning you with holy kisses while you sleep, bursting into chaste flame while the angels keep their awe-hushed watch.

Selah

Lost Sheep

*M*Y LOST LOVES SIT AT THE BOTTOM of the pile, alone and forlorn. They gaze out of windows at white skies that seem empty and uncaring. They wearily climb concrete stairwells with limbs made of lead, weighed down by the sameness and the endless effort. They try everything they can think of to discover love and only find they are curling their lips at the bitter taste of reality.

But there is something, somehow, deep inside each of them, that has not entirely given up hope. That keeps on searching for me in other faces, though they turn away. That believes in goodness, despite seeing it nowhere. That nods to the flowering weed along the wayside, recognizing a soulmate.

These are my lambs, and I will search tirelessly, high and low, in thickets and on precipices, in tenements and shantytowns, dungeons and sweatshops. Each one will be found, and flung over my shoulder, and have their own name breathed into their ear by the Good Shepherd, who knows all their markings, and who sees his wounds in the brands the world has burned into their skin. He will take the heavy weight of all that they are and love it into lightness and carry them home.

Selah

Bicycle

AITH IS LIKE RIDING A BICYCLE ALONG unknown trails. You will never know when the unexpected slope will end, when you can stop for a breather at the crest of a hill before putting your exhausted feet up on the handlebars for a joyous, effortless ride down. You will not see the mud until you are encumbered by it, nor be aware of the puddle on concrete that will wash your wheels clean once you make it onward.

There will be times when you wonder why you started out, and times when you wonder where the finish line is. You will see tracks off to the left and the right of your path and sometimes explore them, coming back again to the main road savaged by brambles or sated by strawberries. The most uneven lane may seem exhilarating, or the smoothest show up its potholes and imperfections more than another, less even section.

Yet all the journey is exactly what it is, and there is no point hankering after earlier places, or wanting to return to the beginning, though you may start over exactly where you are at any time.

When you reach the end, you will have bruises and grazes, but also wide eyes and flushed cheeks. You will be able to say along with all my creation, "I lived."

Selah

Sight

*E*VERY EYE IS A POOL FOR ME TO DIVE INTO. How it receives light is how it receives everything, including me. This is why I am eager to help you remove planks and then splinters, for sight cannot be clear where such impediments exist, and the truth needs open vision to be really seen and appreciated.

When you can see the Light of the World, even though you be blind, you will see by that same Light. For I came to illuminate all things by my grace, and to share understanding and Sophia wisdom with you all.

How the truths and reality of God's kingdom long to be really seen, resounding with all the colours of his glory and reverberating with the echoes of his majesty! For all the holy frequencies of heaven are here and ever before you, the spectrum of light you know, and the hues you can perceive, as well as far beyond these into realms of shade and tone too deep or bright for your young eyes and small seeings.

But keep looking, my lambs, keep searching, always gaze. For even and most especially with your eyes closed in prayer, there is more to see and wonder at than you could ever imagine!

Selah

Blank

*T*URN OFF THE SCREEN, CLOSE THE WINDOWS and tabs vying for your attention. Put the phone face down on the chair, on the table, out of arm's reach. Feel the tugging of something else on your heartstrings and answer its call. What if the next few moments are a blank page, a new beginning? What if how you start them might transfigure how you use your time, how you prioritize life, how you pray?

What if you started listening instead of scrolling? What if you began writing beauty instead of reading reams of the same old tired truisms that, really, you knew anyway? What if?

Ask yourself: What might the next few moments, stolen away with me, bring? Wouldn't you like to start an adventure, feel your wings beginning to lift? Wouldn't it be heaven to just, for a few moments, close your eyes and imagine that other realm?

What if you learned to breathe deeply again, and say my name, over and over, rolling tides of love round and round upon your tongue? What if there were no end to the ideas and the wonder that came flowing out of the stillness that you know is there, that you feel beneath your aching heart? What if you heard my voice urging you to follow me, and threw all your nets, unmended, to one side? I am here, the whispers are waiting, and the blank pages pulse with possibility.

Selah

Heroes

*M*OST HEROES REMAIN UNSUNG. No one tells their tales or puts their names up in lights, nor shines honour upon them. Most true heroes stay small, shrinking away from the vagaries of glory and fame. They would be shocked to know they were living heroic lives, which are worked out in the deep mud of struggle or carrying the load of poverty, the kind that makes your bones ache for the warm, and your feet for the dry.

They somehow straddle pieces of drifting sand and leap where they need to go, taking risks for others, and are never mindful of their own security or of what it might cost them. They are grateful for the little they have and know the right altar at which to offer their thanks.

They give themselves utterly to love and all the sacrifices it asks of them. They adapt their needs to serve those of their sisters and brothers. They are always willing to lay down the desires of their own flesh for the comfort of another, as though they were Raleigh to all the queens and kings they see my children to be.

And these small, these poor, these persevering, consistent lovers of the human soul, these who humbly walk with me, often without knowing it, who uncomplainingly trade ease for misery to further the well-being of others, these are the kings and queens of heaven. And there they will shine, and everyone shall know their names and speak of their great deeds; though the world counts them nothing now, all shall then be made known. For now, and always, their names are writ large in my book of life, and their dear souls are carried precious in the depths of my heart.

Selah

Shore

PROSTRATE YOURSELF HERE BEFORE THE LORD, knocked down to the ground by the outrageous force of grace, your nose pressed into the wet sand. Crouch along on your belly, keeping it one with the earth, with the golden grains, and pay no attention to those with their noses lifted high in the air (who do not see you in any case). They are not the ones to talk to. Instead associate with your fellow sand-crawlers, the ones frequenting the tidal zones, laid so low that their heartbeats press against my shorelines. For here the weak and the helpless know my voice and find joy in my waves and breakers rolling over them.

Here lie the soaked in spirit and the drenched in grace, and here you belong. From this place rises a heart-song so vivid and powerful that it blesses even me. Where better to hear the roar of the ocean, my love, and relate to the wretched, than here, in the danger zone, amongst the fallen? Wriggling with the other sandworms in the glory of sodden shore, with travelling stones bleached white and the empty shells each holding a universe of lament?

Roll here with the rest of the flotsam, sand clumped in your hair, and hear laughter growling, sacred song prowling the seashore, waiting for Christ the Beachcomber to collect his treasures and take them home.

Selah

ACKNOWLEDGEMENTS

Heartfelt thanks go to everyone who has walked alongside me in my faith path or encouraged my writing and creativity.

I am ever grateful for the loving support of Rowan and Gareth. You live in my heart. Also for the love and encouragement from my parents, Val and Graham, and for all the friends and family who have believed in me and valued my contributions despite my constricted life and ill health.

Many thanks to those who read, and commented on early drafts of this book, and those who prayed for or encouraged me, especially Martin Willoughby, Beverly Flanagan, Angela Gordon, Jeannie Kendall, Barbara Boruff, Tanya Neumann, Gill Fuller, Fiona Veitch Smith, and my beloved anam cara, Bev Wilson.

I am deeply appreciative to Richard Rohr and Jen Rees Larcombe for bothering to read pieces by a complete unknown, and for astonishing me by giving me their enthusiastic affirmation, as well of course as for everything they've ever written and all the inspiration they have been in my life.

Thanks also go to Jon M. Sweeney and all at Paraclete Press for working with me to give this offering to the world to read instead of leaving it to languish on my hard drive.

Deep gratitude to my faith guides and mentors: Hugh and Ruth Dibbens, Iain Lothian, James

Grover, Allison Stickler, Sue Robertson, and the Rev. Canon Dennis Winter.

Thank you, too, to two long departed women: my godmother Gwen, who always knew I was a writer, and helped me believe it too. And to Mrs Ghent, who, when I was nine, let me write and paint to my heart's content in class every day for a year, once I'd finished my maths.

KEREN DIBBENS-WYATT is a contemplative and mystic in the Christian tradition with a passion for prayer and creativity. She writes to encourage others into knowing the Lord more intimately, as well as to share the poetic ponderings of her heart. She suffers from M.E. (myalgic encephalomyelitis), which sadly keeps her mostly housebound, often confined to bed, and largely out of the trouble she would get into otherwise. She lives in southeast England with her poet husband and their odd but delightful black and white cat.

Keren also writes prayers, poetry, theology, and fiction and has recently discovered a talent for painting in pastels which she enjoys immensely, and other interests when she has the energy include short bursts of reading, photography, and crocheting things that inevitably come out wonky. You can connect with Keren at her website, www .kerendibbenswyatt.com, or on social media.

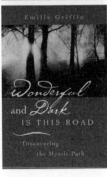